THE LUNATIC DIARIES

THE LUNATIC DIARIES

RANDOM NOTES FROM BIZCOMICS

Written by Mark Nelson O'Brien
Illustrated by Nate Fakes

Published by BizComics: bizcomics.club
ISBN: 1983546968
ISBN-13: 9781983546969

DEDICATION

We dedicate this book to anyone who's ever had a creative urge, anyone who's ever had an unorthodox thought, anyone who's ever had an unyielding dream, and everyone who's ever served in the mad, maddening, mysterious, and magnificently marvelous milieu of marketing.

CONTENTS

ACKNOWLEDGMENTS

Mark would like to thank his wife, Anne, for teaching him by example how to love unconditionally; Nate for teaching him how to remain inspired; Sammy (his cat) for teaching him to be peaceful; Eddie (his dog) for teaching him to be happy; and God for the ability to think as he does (make of that what you will) and for the gift of writing that lets him inflict his thinking on the rest of the world.

Nate would like to thank his family, especially his wife Kelsey, his daughter Ella, and his cat, Tiger, for continuing to support a cartoonist through all the craziness throughout his career; Mark, without whose awesome accompanying words to go with the comics this book would have never been made; JoAnna Bennett and Jonathan Spiliotopoulos of O'Brien Communications Group for all the BizComics meetings and sharing this vision; and The Big Guy in the sky: God, I thank you as well for, well, everything (but in this case, mostly humor).

INTRODUCTION

In early 2013, O'Brien Communications Group had the notion to create a monthly comic strip to promote its work and to share the humorous absurdity that comes with that work as part of the human condition. With an unlimited source of material with which to write the strips, all that remained was to find an illustrator.

Enter Nate Fakes, a young man who'd already established a reputation for his work with *Mad* magazine and various syndicated outlets. Mark wrote an initial strip and sent it to Nate. Nate illustrated it with his characteristic brilliance and his uncanny ability to tell an entire story in a single facial expression. And in May of 2013, the first *Thought Leadership* strip was published. It continues to this day.

Then, in June of 2015, a conversation took place that would change the course of world history. Well ... maybe not the history of the whole world. But it would certainly change the lives and the histories of the two clowns who participated in the conversation.

Here's the entirety of that conversation, transcribed for posterity, enshrined in the Library of Congress, and buried in a time capsule in Mildew, Alabama, to be disinterred at the point (in history, of course) at which someone down there discovers (or re-invents) the shovel:

Nate: "Hi, Mark. It's Nate."
Mark: "Hi, Nate."
Nate: "Do you know cartoons can be used for marketing?"
Mark: "The thought had crossed my mind."
Nate: "Why don't we create a business to use cartoons in marketing?"
Mark: "You mean like BizComics?"
Nate: "Like what?"
Mark: "Never mind."

The rest, as they say, is history ... but not necessarily world history.

From that day forward, we went dutifully and diligently about the business of marketing BizComics. We wrote (to date) almost 100 blog posts, every one of which was accompanied (or inspired) by an original cartoon. We sent emails to a large and growing list of people and companies every two weeks. We got a little interest from Costco (they picked up one cartoon for their Facebook page). We sent two proposals to Baker & Taylor (the book distributor), for the purpose of reviving the two cats (named Baker and Taylor) immortalized by Jan Louch in her book, *The True Tails of Baker and Taylor.* We created exhaustive lists of industries, identified people at companies within each of them, and called or emailed all of them. Our efforts earned us one case of carpal tunnel syndrome and two cauliflower ears. And they gave us the opportunity to learn some very valuable lessons.

We learned to believe in our talents. We learned to believe in the creative quality and caliber of the work. We learned to believe in our aptitudes to create a supply of exceptional and differentiating ideas and content. We learned to believe in and rely on each other. We learned — and came to fully appreciate — this wisdom from Ralph Waldo Emerson's 1841 essay, "Self-Reliance":

> To believe our own thought, to believe that what is true for you in your private heart is true for all men — that is genius ... A man should learn to detect and watch that gleam of light which flashes across his mind from within ... Yet he dismisses without notice his thought, because it is his ... Great works of art have no more affecting lesson for us than this. They teach us to abide by our spontaneous impression with good-humored inflexibility — then most when the whole cry of voices is on the other side. Else, to-morrow a stranger will say with masterly good sense precisely what we have thought and felt all the time, and we shall be forced to take with shame our own opinion from another.

We don't mean to suggest we're geniuses, by any stretch. (Our spouses will vouch for that.) And we're not presumptuous enough to consider the work we produced for BizComics to be art. But because both of us tend to break out in hives when we take our own opinions from others, it seemed prudent and sensible to publish our work before someone else ... uh ... liberated it, so to speak.

The book you hold in your hand manifests our determination to share, as Emerson put it, what we have thought and felt. It reflects the ways in which we see the world. Since you're now the proud owner of *The Lunatic Diaries: Volume One*, we hope it compels you to think in ways other than the ways in which you'd be otherwise inclined or prompted to think. And we hope it makes you smile.

We sincerely thank you for buying this book. It's our honor to share this work of our hearts and our imaginations with you. We hope you enjoy it. Especially if you enjoy it, we hope to continue to create work that means something to us. If it means something to you, as well, we're all the more grateful.

Mark Nelson O'Brien
Nate Fakes
February 28, 2018

ABOVE THE FOLD

In the days in which Superman was still flying high on TV, in which Clark Kent was still managing to fool everyone with a disguise that comprised only a pair of glasses, and in which newspapers were the medium in which most people consumed daily information, most newspapers (with the possible exception of tabloids) were folded. Consequently, important stories (in the opinion of the editors) appeared on the top half of the paper — or above the fold.

But those days are gone now. So are misguided notions of placing your important content (in the opinion of your boss) above some imaginary fold on your website.

If you want to test the fallacy of the notion of the fold on websites, try these three simple tests:

1. The illusory fold will be determined by a combination of your browser, your screen size, and your screen resolution. Measure the size of your screen diagonally, from the bottom left to the top right. Make note of the measurement.

   Log into your control panel and select any resolution you want. Make note of your selection. By any criteria you want to use, determine where you think the fold is.

   Now go back into the control panel and change the resolution. Lather, rinse, repeat. Good luck.
2. Fold your monitor anywhere you want to, making sure the horizontal crease is even. Anything that appears above the crease is above the fold. Anything that appears below the crease is below the fold.
3. Go to any website created after Al Gore invented responsive design. If you can definitively determine which of the panels on that site appear above the fold and which ones appear below, please let us know.

Okay. We're joking. If the design of your site is done artfully enough — if the content is presented with enough white space to let it and your readers breathe, enough absence of clutter — visitors do read sites from the top down and will consume the content at the top of your site before they consume the consent below it. But we really do need to get over our allegiance to the fold.

Clear Vision

Establishing a clear vision for your company reminds us of the old saying: "If it were easy, everyone would do it."

In truth, it's not easy to establish a clear vision for any company. Given the accelerating pace of everything, we tend to incline toward assuming any idea, relentlessly communicated through ever-proliferating media, will necessarily produce the proverbial rainbow-ending pot of gold. Not so much.

Here's all you need to know about creating a clear vision:

- It takes critical thinking, which fewer and fewer people seem inclined to invest.
- It takes time, which fewer and fewer people seem inclined to spend on anything.

- It takes the hard work of determining strategic objectives, in which fewer and fewer people seem inclined to engage.
- It takes clear articulation of persuasive messages, the crafting of which fewer and fewer people seem capable.

At risk of seeming to be reductive or prescriptive, we have some humble suggestions for tackling the time-consuming, thought-intensive, strategic, persuasive work of establishing a vision:

First, think about why you're doing what you're doing. Are you filling a need? Are you taking advantage of an opportunity? Are you appealing to a particular market or segment of a market? Why will you succeed?

Second, stop whatever you think you should be doing. If everyone could do what you're trying to do, it would have been done before. Before you begin again, take stock of why you're doing what you're doing. Since you're the one who's doing it, how and why is the way you're doing it different? In what ways is it better? Why should your prospects choose you?

Third, if you can't explain why you're doing something, don't do it. As another old saying goes: "If you don't know where you're going, any road will get you there." Your business is too important to put it at the mercy of that kind of waywardness.

Finally, make sure you know your target audience(s) well enough to speak their language. What's important to you may not be important to them. And if they don't think you care about selling to them, they definitely won't care about buying from you.

If you do those four things, you'll have established a clear vision for your company. You'll also have set its direction and given it its best shot at success.

If you can see clearly now, so can your prospects.

BELLS AND WHISTLES

If you have a marketing website, especially a B2B marketing site, it has two jobs:

- To direct sensory and mechanical responses.
- To direct those responses into your sales channel.

It has to do those two jobs by doing four other things, in this order:

1. Make it readily apparent what's being offered and by whom.
2. Present additional information clearly and accessibly.
3. Make it easy for visitors to contact and/or follow you in social media.
4. Make them an offer they can't refuse.

They need to be done in that order because that's what visitors want. Contrary to popular expectation, B2B visitors aren't likely to arrive at your site because of keyword cleverness, density, or selection. SEO is all but immaterial.

Rather, visitors arrive because they search for a name — a company name, a product name, a service name, or an individual's name. Site statistics show 95 to 98 percent of traffic on B2B sites arrives by such searches. And the higher the price point of what you're selling, the lower the likelihood of keyword-driven traffic.

A site designed to optimize the four precepts above will be clean, uncluttered, accessible, and neither exhaustive nor exhausting. Websites don't need to be packed with everything you can think to put it in them — only enough to get your prospects interested enough to want to talk with you.

Form (design) needs to follow function (purpose). It needs to serve presentation and navigation. Words and images for their own sake might be art. But words and images employed to follow function to accomplish the achievement of business objectives have to be purposefully, deliberately, effectively designed.

Likewise, form and function have to be separated from gimmicks. Website design isn't a tchotchke fair; although, many designers see websites as opportunities to flaunt their cyber trinkets. Adding clutter to a website adds insult (bad sense) to injury (bad design).

Simplicity, subtlety, cleanliness, uncomplicated navigation, accessible presentation, and uncluttered sensory and mechanical responses. Create your website to fulfill those criteria, and your visitors will have the experience they want — not the bells and whistles you may want to give them.

THE MEDIUM NEED NOT BE THE MESSAGE

Far be it from us to question the intellectual acuity (to say nothing of the foresight) of the late Marshall McLuhan. But we have to wonder if he'd have thought the medium is the message if he were still with us today.

It seems to us, halfway through the second decade of the 21st century, media have become so prolific, the number of messages so profuse, and the speed with which media and messages proliferate that there's simply no time to reflect on the longer term implications of media or messages — the structural, cultural, and social changes they engender:

- Will Twitter's forcing us to compress expression into 140 characters precipitate changes in the ways in which we think, in the ways in which we communicate in other media?
- Will the proliferation of business jargon like authentic, best of breed, disruption, innovation, socialize, solution, touchpoint, and other terms yield a kind of ill-defined verbal shorthand devoid of any meaning, let alone shared meaning?
- Will the emergence of self-driving cars have any profound effects on life expectancy, mortality tables, the habits of pedestrians, or our willingness to put our lives in the figurative hands of pre-programmed and utterly dispassionate algorithms?

Who cares?

If all we're interested in is the clear communication of messages intended to engage, entertain, and educate, we got your medium right here.

Comics are the perfect medium in which to express almost anything. They can grab attention with their content, verbal and visual. They can be pointed, funny, and/or irreverent. They can be informative, without being preachy or pedantic. And they can indicate the fact that you don't take yourself too seriously, even as they demonstrate that you know your stuff cold.

Most important, they render the media in which they appear all but irrelevant. Print, web, email, Twitter, LinkedIn, Facebook, mobile, or desktop, it doesn't matter where your cartoons appear. They'll deliver the same message, the same way, to the people you want to reach, regardless of their bandwidth, their headspace, or their attention spans.

Your medium may need life insurance. But with comics, your message won't.

Finding Your Target Audience

Sometimes it may seem as if finding your target audience requires some kind of specialized sleuthing. It doesn't. It does, however, require a little science, a little art, and a little self-faith. Here some suggestions for applying all three:

Science

Depending on what you intend to sell, you may or may not need to conduct any formal market research. For example:

- If you're going to sell adhesive dressings for everyday cuts and scrapes, you might not need extensive research on your target market (people with everyday cuts and scrapes). You will, however, face some pretty stiff competition from Band-Aid.
- On the other hand, if you're going to sell curare-tipped arrows for hunting maned wolves in eastern Bolivia, you might have to do a fair bit of homework to identify the purchasing members of your target audience.

Art

Depending on whether you're reasonably comfortable you know your target audience — or that you've done adequate research to identify it — you can be creative. If you can present your message in ways the members of your target audience aren't likely to have seen or aren't likely to expect, you're quite likely to engage them enough to deliver your message. And if you manage to entertain and educate them, you'll probably grab some mindshare in the bargain.

Self-Faith

Depending on your ability to trust yourself, your judgment, and your ability to relate to your target audience, self-faith may be the most important aspect of finding your target audience. To paraphrase Abraham Lincoln, "You can reach all the people some of the time, and some of the people all the time, but you cannot reach all the people all the time."

If you recognize and accept the fact that those who think as you do will relate to the ways in which you communicate, you'll effectively attract the members of your target audience most likely to establish a rapport with you and your brand — and to trust what you're selling enough to buy it.

It may not always be easy to find your target audience. But letting comics do it will be less expensive and more effective than hiring a detective agency.

POP-UP ADS

Pop-up ads were always annoying. Now they're unscrupulous and arguably dangerous, too. Considering the fact that pop-up ads have rendered themselves all but useless, they're also completely unnecessary. And they may even be insulting. Maybe that's why they're spawning something like a closet industry dedicated to blocking or removing them.

Part of this is easy enough to understand: Social media changed the marketing-communication game. Before social media, marketing employed one or both of two strategies: push and/or pull. By fostering the proliferation of content — and by leaving it up to consumers of media to select the content they want to consume — social media effectively nullified push. And pop-up ads are the quintessential push tactic, which is why they're as alienating as they are distracting.

What's hard to understand is why. Why would marketers think they have to employ pop-up ads (or any other push tactics, for that matter)? If the brands they're marketing have the authority to tell their own persuasive stories, why do marketers think they need to assault consumers' senses with the cyber equivalent of the Louisville Slugger, rather then pulling them in more gently with persuasive, palatable content that's the cyber equivalent of the Nerf Bat? Darned if we know.

And here's the most confounding part: With the web, we're talking about a medium that's already begotten banner blindness, a phenomenon in which we no longer see anything our increasingly conditioned powers of perception perceive as advertising. So much for push. In that sense, pop-up advertising would seem to be a kind of self-defeating doubling down: "Well, if banner ads torqued 'em off, wait'll they get a load of pop-up ads."

The good news is we don't have to create or rely on pop-up advertising. As long as we're creating meaningful content — and packaging it attractively and persuasively — we'll be pulling the members of our target audiences effectively. And if we're using the combination of content and packaging to engage, educate, and entertain, we'll be ahead of the game. So will our consumers.

In that sense, purveyors of pop-up ads might be considered the new pushers.

ALL ADVERTISING IS NOT CREATED EQUAL

Yes. Ad blockers are wreaking havoc on web advertising. No. Advertising is not dead, ad blockers and perilous predictions for print notwithstanding. But it is sucking wind a bit. And it may have nothing to blame but itself.

Consider native advertising. If you're not familiar with the term, here's an excerpt from *Wikipedia:*

> Native advertising is a form of online advertising that matches the form and function of the platform on which it appears.

Why? If a brand has the authority to tell its story, why does it need to match form and function (translation: disguise or camouflage itself) by playing chameleon to its chosen media? Why can't it stand on its own? Has anyone asked the user if native advertising provides utility and added value?

Now consider programmatic advertising. If that's a new one on you, here's an excerpt from "WTF is programmatic advertising?":

> "Programmatic" ad buying typically refers to the use of software to purchase digital advertising, as opposed to the traditional process that involves RFPs, human negotiations and manual insertion orders. It's using machines to buy ads, basically.

Got that? Programmatic advertising employs algorithmic programs to read the data from marketing-automation software and uses said data to automate the acquisition of advertising media intended to appeal to the personae marketing automation software use as proxies for target customers. What could go wrong?

And then there's outdoor advertising. While the jury may be out on the distracting effects of billboards on driving, there's one group for which they're simply a non-factor: seniors. That's right. According to media research we conducted in the course of promoting a senior-living community, billboards have almost no effectiveness for pitching golden-agers because those folks just don't see them. Why? They're keeping their eyes on the road, proving once and for all that wisdom does come with age.

Don't give up on advertising. But use it wisely. Since not all of it is created equal, it requires judicious use in deliberately select media. Most important, it requires realistic expectations.

Oh ... and keep your eyes on the road.

ARE YOU ENGAGED?

We don't mean to suggest we want to propose marriage. Rather, we're inquiring whether you — or, more specifically your brand — are engaged in two important ways with two equally important but very different audiences.

The first audience to consider comprises your employees. Are they engaged with your brand? Do they know what it represents? If you asked any number of them what the brand means, would all of them give you the same answer? Have they personalized it; that is, have they connected with it in ways that enable them to feel like its representatives in their day-to-day activities? How do you know?

Allowing your employees to be engaged with your brand begins with clearly communicating your vision. Your vision — the articulation of what you want your organization to become — is the first step toward establishing the direction of your organization, as well as its culture, its personality, and its differentiating value propositions.

The second audience to consider comprises every one of your prospects. They, too, have to be engaged with your brand. They can be reached in a variety of media, social and otherwise. And, cost notwithstanding, no medium should be off the table.

God invented LinkedIn, Facebook, Twitter, Reddit, Scoop.it, Digg, RSS, and every other platform and website by which to spread your word to be used. Will they all be effective? No. Can they all be employed for next to nothing? Yes. Is it worth the risk of skipping media outlets if they have the potential to convert one prospect into a customer? Positively not.

As the cartoon suggests, if you and your employees aren't engaged with your brand, you're probably not ready to engage others — particularly your prospects — with your brand. And you're surely not ready to engage social media in the positioning and promotion of your brand. But as undertakings go, this one's not momentous.

If you've started with your vision and cascaded it down through your organization, you're already on the right track. With your employees fully engaged, then, you'll be ready to engage your prospects through social media channels, secure in the knowledge that their every interaction with every one of your employees will represent your brand consistently.

You can take that as a proposal, if you like.

A Happy Medium

You can't blame folks for being confused about media. Terms from one medium — like banners from outdoor advertising — transfer to another medium — like banners for web advertising — almost as fast as new media emerge. It'd be hard enough to keep up if media were the only things changing. But change seems to define the whole world as much as anything else these days.

The effectiveness of banner ads continues its decline. What would we expect from a medium that yielded its own phenomenon: banner blindness? The fact is, if you have bigger marketing fish to fry, the medium is a red herring. (Ouch!) You're better served by concentrating on just two things — your message and its packaging.

Let's say you're a web-development firm that wants to emphasize the importance of tracking site traffic and responding constructively to user behavior by enhancing content that's being accessed and eliminating content that's not. You could consider media — say web or print — and create an ad that says this: "It's important to track site traffic and respond constructively to user behavior by enhancing content that's being accessed and eliminating content that's not."

Or you could consider the message — that you ignore traffic statistics and user behavior at the risk of your business — and package it engagingly, like this:

The medium then becomes secondary. And you can select any medium based on a criterion as simple as budget: If you can afford print, use print. If you can only afford web advertising, use the web. Or if you want to minimize your spend and maximize your targeting, use email and a select list of prospects.

One more thing: If you really want to engage, consider using humor. We seem to be losing our senses of humor as rapidly as media are proliferating. Don't let it happen. If you use humor in your communications, regardless of medium, you'll have fun creating your messages. And your prospects will have fun reading them.

You Have To Do the Work

Miles Davis once said there's only one in every 50 performances in which musicians play beyond themselves, in which they transcend their technical abilities and their imaginations to play from pure, unconscious inspiration. But it's the other 49 performances by which musicians earn the right to call themselves professionals. And so it is for all of us.

We all have aspirations to create the video, the ad, the comic, the letter, the email, or the meme that goes viral. But our chances of getting there are slim. And we still have products and services to sell, clients to represent, brands to position and promote, and work to do. It's only in getting that work done — by going about our jobs with diligence and fastidiousness — that we earn the right to call ourselves professionals.

So, if we shouldn't spend our professional time and effort trying to go viral, what should we do?

1. Learn everything we can about:
   - The products and services we have to sell
   - The clients we represent
   - Their businesses and their brands
   - The industries they serve
   - Their target audiences
2. Get to work:
   - Create content with which to communicate those products and services
   - Treat our clients' businesses and their brands as our own
   - Determine the media in which their industries communicate
   - Speak the language of their consumers sincerely and persuasively
3. Aspire to perfection.

Wait. Aspire to perfection?

That's right. Aspiring to perfection doesn't mean we'll be perfect any more than aspiring to going viral will ensure we'll achieve virality. But if we're not working to the best of our abilities every day, if we're not striving to achieve something beyond ourselves, to transcend our technical abilities and our imaginations — even if we don't get there — on what grounds do we earn the right to call ourselves professionals?

So, go ahead. Give it your best shot. Even if you don't achieve perfection, you can be proud anyway, knowing you've done the work.

For most of us, the closest we'll get to going viral is catching the flu. Try anyway.

ESCAPING THE HERD

We have three divisions: a sensational division, a mediocre division, and a rotten division. The sensational division is on the top floor ... There aren't too many clients who want to operate in that rarefied atmosphere. In the mediocre division, we have clients who compromise: Put in some sensational ingredients, some rotten ones, and you have the opportunity to do mediocre work. The rotten division is where the bulk of the work is — and the reason it's rotten is that clients determine the product.
(HERB LUBALIN)

Most brand owners share the myopic inability to see their own brands. They're too close to them to be able to see them clearly and to perceive them objectively from the perspectives of their prospects. Nevertheless, many brand owners resist the introduction of that kind of optical clarity or perspectival objectivity. When presented with the new, they try as they might to revert to the old.

Is change really that fearsome?

Why is that objectivity perceived as threatening? It's not just brands that are at stake. It's work, reputations, and integrity. In theory, brand owners rely on others to ensure their brands are neither diluted nor diminished. But as Albert Einstein correctly observed, "In theory, theory and practice are the same. In practice, they're different."

Would we tell contractors how to build our homes? Would we tell software developers how to develop applications? Would we tell manufacturers how to machine parts? Would we tell dentists how to drill and fill? No. It wouldn't occur to us.

Nevertheless, we tell the people we hire to position and manage our brands, "Make that blue instead of green." "Select another image." "Choose another word. I don't know that one." "Move the navigation bar on the website." "Say *solution* instead of *product*." Say *innovation* or *disruption* instead of *change*." Why do we do that?

Have we done the research they have? Have we studied the usability and readability studies they have? Do we understand the implications of design, color, and symbolism as they do? Do we assess the market and audience behaviors as they do before they select a color, design a thing, or write a word?

No. We don't. Nor should we.

If we're going to hire brand consultants, we should trust them — and let them separate us from the herd.

People First

We tend to meet any new situation by reorganizing; and a wonderful method it can be for creating the illusion of progress while producing confusion, inefficiency, and demoralization.
(Charlton Ogburn, 1911-1998)

We once worked with a company that hired a consulting professor from a prestigious university to help it with an organizational transformation. The professor had written a book on the subject. The transformation was to be accomplished in just 90 days.

All employees, regardless of title or responsibility, were assigned to cross-departmental, cross-disciplinary teams. Each team was given a process to transform. Their ideas blazed like wildfire — operational improvements, process-engineering concepts, and counter-orthodox proposals. The only thing hotter than the ideas was the enthusiasm they generated.

Based on those ideas, the organization was operationally re-evaluated and completely restructured. Most of the employees were given new roles and responsibilities. But ...

On the morning after, the company was despondently dysfunctional. Productivity tanked. Product development was fitful. Responsiveness declined, along with customer satisfaction. Everyone who'd known to whom to turn for knowledge and support in their old positions lost all their lifelines in their new ones.

The CEO expressed his bewilderment and anger at people for not performing. His idea of change was that it should be top down, driven only by and comfortable only to him. So, heads started to roll, exacerbating the problem by introducing insecurity into an environment of unfamiliarity and uncertainty.

Throwing folks into the deep end may seem like a sound, hard-nosed management approach. But it reflects disrespect for people and disregard for their humanity.

Organizational transformation begins with people, not processes. Had the company known that, its reorganization would have been fluid, rather than rigid. People would have slid more productively into functional position, rather than being force-fit into mandatory line. They would have adapted to and improved new processes, rather than running blindly along with processes they didn't understand. And they would have been able to forge alliances with their new positional colleagues as they transitioned in, rather than being left without safety nets when they were pushed out on the wire.

The effects of overlooking your people are neither pretty nor productive. And the only thing that suffers more than your people when they're ignored is your brand.

People first. Always people first.

Not Quite That Direct

direct (adjective):

1. *straightforward, direct, candid*
2. *without intervening persons, influences, factors, etc.; immediate; personal*

Uh … we'd like to have a word with you about direct marketing.

We've seen fit to include the pertinent definitions of direct here because, at times, direct marketers are inclined to take them too literally, causing those marketers to be a tad too … well … direct.

We don't want to be misunderstood: Directness definitely has its place. But it should be exercised in the derivation of your messages, in the presentation of your value propositions, and in the language with which you communicate. It should not be exercised in the spamming, strafing, or otherwise browbeating your prospects into a state of vanquished apathy.

Everyone who creates a product or develops a service thinks it's the greatest thing since the beer bong. That's as it should be. But it doesn't mean the world shares your opinion. The bitter pill is — unless you've cured cancer or figured out what the hell's up with Donald Trump's hair — no one cares.

That's right. You're the sole proprietor of the conviction that the world should beat a path to your bank account. But it doesn't mean you can beat the world into buying what you're selling.

Research your market. Identify the need you'll fill. Plot your objectives. Identify your value propositions. Craft your messages clearly. Package them engagingly and persuasively. (Comics are engaging. They also can be entertaining and educational, if we do say so ourselves.) Select your media strategically. Communicate persistently — even relentlessly — but do it politely and gently.

In these, the Ages of Social Media and Content Marketing, the members of your target audience(s) select the content they want to consume. Pull them in enticingly. They're not going to be pushed into anything anymore. And they're certainly not going to be bullied.

Be proud of what you've created. Put your best foot forward in promoting what you've created. And by all means, be direct. But put down the hammer, even if it's only a figurative one.

Remember the proverb: If your only tool is an anvil, every problem has to be a horseshoe ... or something like that.

No Fighting Chance

straitjacket (noun)

- *garment made of strong material and designed to bind the arms*
- *anything that severely confines, constricts, or hinders*

straitjacket (verb)

- *to put in or as in a straitjacket*

Scenario A. Imagine you're a gym owner who wants to cultivate a stable of mixed martial arts fighters. Imagine one of those fighters shows undeniable potential, winning all of his matches leading up to the inevitable championship fight. Imagine you tell him your strategy for the fight is to tie his right wrist to his left ankle and pull both of them up behind his back. Then imagine you tell him you expect him not just to fight like that — you expect him to win.

That's so crazy as to be laughably dismissible, right? Not so fast. Consider this:

Scenario B: Imagine you're a business owner who wants to cultivate a stable, credible, prominent, recognizable, memorable, trusted brand. Imagine you hire a creative team that shows undeniable potential, winning all of its client engagements leading up to the inevitable re-staging of your brand. Imagine you tell the team your strategy for the re-positioning is to conform to everything you like, even though you're unable to define clearly what you like, provide clear examples of what you like, or give clear explanations for why you like what you like. Then imagine you tell the team members you expect them not just to adhere to everything you like — you expect them to succeed.

Far fetched? Not so much.

If you've hired a creative team, you must at least suspect you're not the target audience. You must at least have some awareness of your creative limitations. You must at least have some inkling that your ability to differentiate your brand from the brands of your competitors might be lacking in some way. But you just ... can't ... let ... AAAAARRRRRRGGGGGGHHHHH!!!!!!!

Relax. If you handcuff, hamstring, hogtie, or otherwise hinder your creative team, you won't give them a fighting chance.

The moral of the story? Stay out of the octagon. You and your brand might get knocked out.

GET OVER IT

TRIGGER WARNING: THE FOLLOWING MESSAGE CONTAINS CONTENT THAT MAY BE UPSETTING TO THOSE WITH MISPLACED SENSES OF PRIORITY, MISGUIDED IMPRESSIONS OF THEIR TARGET AUDIENCES, MISBEGOTTEN NOTIONS ABOUT MARKETING, MISTAKEN SENSES OF THEIR OWN IMPORTANCE, AND/OR BALLOONING EGOS!

You know that logo you love so much? No one else cares about it anywhere near as much as you do.

Yes. It's your graphic identity. It's the mark of your business. It's the emblem of your brand. It's the reflection of your brand's personality. It's symbolic of the promise you make to your customers and your prospects. And nobody cares.

Why should they? There are only two contexts in which your logo is likely to appear. The size of the thing isn't material to your success in either of them:

1. You haven't yet established any brand awareness. If no one knows who you are, what you're selling, and why it's any good, you should be establishing your credibility and persuading people to buy what you're selling instead of showing them how big your logo can be.
2. You've already established your brand so effectively you've achieved household-name status. If everybody knows who you are, the size of your logo isn't going to persuade people to buy any more of what you're selling. You should be convincing them to buy more of it, whatever it is.

That's right. The only thing your customers and prospects care about is how you communicate the value of your brand — and how you fulfill your brand's promise with reliable quality and consistent delivery.

But take heart. If you're still of a mind to expand the size of your logo, you can take advantage of a handy extension for Google's Chrome browser. And if the size of your logo — no matter how big it is — isn't enough to let your customers and prospects know what you think is important (as opposed to what they think is important), perhaps you'll be able to derive some satisfaction from knowing you at least have your own song, "Make the Logo Bigger", which you can find on YouTube.

And if none of that works, you may just have to content yourself with cuing up another song, the Eagles' "Get Over It", and turning it up loud enough to offend people with the volume, rather than with the size of your logo.

Burning the Candle at Both Ends

The story you're about to read is true. The names have been changed to protect the hapless.

We recently tried to help a gentleman (we'll call him The Franchisee) who bought a franchise from a company (we'll call it The Franchisor). The Franchisor promised The Franchisee the space he'd leased would be 40-percent occupied when he opened. (It wasn't.) The Franchisor promised The Franchisee it would provide adequate outdoor signage. (It didn't.) The Franchisor promised The Franchisee it would be responsive to his needs. (It wasn't.)

On the bright side, The Franchisee was given the privilege of forking over a number somewhere in the mid-six-figures for the honor of operating under the name of The Franchisor. In exchange for The Franchisee's investment, The Franchisor, thereafter, in good faith:

- Gave The Franchisee no marketing support
- Required The Franchisee to pay $10,000 to The Franchisor's captive advertising agency
- Allowed The Franchisee a single web page, the links from which directed all traffic to The Franchisor
- Prohibited The Franchisee from creating his own website to promote his own location, even if the website positioned The Franchisee's location as a wholly owned franchise of The Franchisor, with a link to The Franchisor's website
- Suggested The Franchisee send out direct-mail postcards, to be purchased from the captive advertising agency, every six weeks for the bargain-basement rate of $700 apiece
- Encouraged The Franchisee to buy Facebook advertising, which would point to The Franchisees' web page, from which The Franchisor would neither derive nor report any meaningful traffic statistics.

So. What did our friend, The Franchisee, do? He did what any other self-respecting businessperson would do given the same set of circumstances: He went broke.

If you believe resources are finite — or if you're of the conviction that you can't spend money you don't have, particularly for no return — you'll be working from an affordable, strategic marketing plan with direct lines to achievable, tactical results.

If, on the other hand, you're not encumbered by reality — or if you're of the conviction that money comes from some inextinguishable source requiring no generation — The Franchisor's business model is flawless.

See you on Facebook.

Somewhere Uber the Rainbow

Somewhere over the rainbow, way up high
There's a land that I've heard of once in a lullaby.
Somewhere over the rainbow, skies are blue
And the dreams that you dare to dream,
Really do come true.

It's only a matter of time before The Great Uberification of Everything reaches sales. We can see it now:

Party A wants to sell Zooger B to Party C. Party A contracts with independent (and likely inexperienced) Party D to sell Zooger B to Party C. Party E (an experienced sales organization) files suit against Party A and Party D for unfair competition. Meanwhile, Zooger B goes unsold. And Party C never gets the zooger it wanted to buy, leaving the pot of gold at the end of the rainbow empty.

Someday I'll wish upon a star
And wake up where the clouds are far behind me.
Where troubles melt like lemon drops,
Way above the chimney tops,
That's where you'll find me.

If you're selling consumer commodities, or inexpensive widgets that require no meaningful expenditures or capital investments, you're good. But if you're selling anything that falls into a sold-not-bought category (financial services, anyone?), not so much. That's because there's a discipline involved that on-demand sales simply can't provide, starting with a strategy — beyond "Sell this now" — that connects the selling organization to its fulfillment activities (sales).

The organization's strategy is its reason for being: "We recognize that, and we can capitalize by creating this." The brand is the manifestation of this in the marketplace. The strategic marketing plan is the means by which this does that. The tactical marketing program is the means by which the strategic plan is actualized. Lead generation is the first sales activity. Qualification is the second sales activity.

Conversion is the third sales activity. And no Uberman is going to connect strategy to conversion.

If you think Uberification will drive sales, you're not in Kansas anymore, Toto.

Somewhere over the rainbow, blue birds fly
Birds fly over the rainbow
Why then, oh why can't I?

(Music and lyrics by Harold Arlen and E.Y. Harburg)

Perception is Not Reality

You have to wonder at the logic (or lack thereof) and the personalities of VPs of Sales, VPs of Sales & Marketing (why do companies give people responsibility for sales AND marketing?), Sales Directors, Sales Managers, and others responsible for running sales organizations. Granted, they have bosses, like the rest of us, who want information now and results yesterday. But you still have to wonder.

Their logic must go something like this: I have to constantly beat my people up to deliver forecasts, lead lists, qualified-prospect lists, sales-call schedules, expense reports, budget plans, expense-against-budget projections, and expense-against-budget-against-forecasted-revenue reports. I also have to hound them relentlessly to update SalesForce, Insightly, Pipedrive, Infusionsoft, TeamSupport, Marketo, Freshdesk, Prophet, NetSuite, Spiceworks, PlanPlus, Five9, PipelineDeals, Hatchbuck, Really Simple Systems, Workbooks, LeadMaster, Base, ProsperWorks, Yogi, Boo Boo, and every other CRM system or database by which they justify their existences so I can justify mine. And if I do that, everything will be somewhere in the range of Hunky Dory to Peachy.

Their personalities are even more fascinating: They have to be some inscrutable combinations of Type A neurotics, wishful thinkers, cockeyed optimists, and abject deniers of reality. Otherwise, they'd realize — with all of the forecasting, lead listing, qualified-prospect listing, sales-call scheduling, expense reporting, budget planning, expense-against-budget projecting, and expense-against-budget-against-forecasted-revenue reporting they're compelling their salespeople to do — the salespeople don't have time to make sales calls or sales. It's no wonder the folks who run sales organizations are more adept at covering their tracks than Tonto.

So, how do we make the heads of sales organizations less reality-averse and more effective? Darned if we know. If it were up to us, the best we could do is offer a few rational suggestions:

- We'd let sales managers manage and report.
- We'd let salespeople sell.
- We'd let sales managers and salespeople use their tools, instead of being used by them.
- And we'd tell the truth, rather than turning sales reporting into creative exercises, Kemosabe.

We do, of course, recognize how naïve that is. And we're very much aware of this:

If rationality were easy, everybody would do it.

GO FLATTER YOURSELF

We read an article in *Fast Company* one time. It was entitled: "How To Become The Most Well-Liked Person In The Office". It said this, in part:

> The relationships you have with the people you work with can make the difference between a great day and a terrible one.

We have to admit to being a little taken aback at the whole concept. It's not that the notion of wanting to be the most well-liked person in the office is so narcissistically absurd. (It is.) It's not the fact that the very title suggests a level of superficiality that makes *Us Weekly* look substantive. (It's not.) It's not the fact that it suggests a degree of self-absorption so culturally pervasive it nullifies the possibility that work can be its own reward. (It can. But we've apparently ruled that possibility out.)

No. What threw us for a nearly irrecoverable loop was the fact that the idea of being the most well-liked person in the office had never occurred to us.

Did we miss something? We certainly concede the importance and the value of relationships. After all, few if any of us would choose to be a Bartleby. And we're well aware that teamwork is bandied about at least as much as any other entry in the corporate lexicon. But how did we overlook the fact that popularity became so important it's now the stuff of business publications?

We still remember fondly those golden days of yesteryear, in which it was a privilege to be hired. It was an honor to do one's work. It was a source of pride to succeed at that work. It was more important to be professional than it was to be well liked. And one of the surest ways to be well liked was to do a good job.

Those days are gone. We're starting to feel very much alone.

We really hope you have terrific relationships at work. And we really hope every day is a great day for you. But if you have a terrible day on occasion, like the rest of us — especially if it's because you failed to be the most well-liked person in the office — go flatter yourself.

IMPRESSIONISTIC CHAOS

When we develop websites for our clients, we diligently test compatibility with all manner of browsers — Firefox, Chrome, Opera, Safari, Torch, Maxthon, SeaMonkey, Avant, Huey, Dewey, Louie, and Popeye. When we've confidently determined the sites render optimally on all browsers — running on desktop, laptop, and mobile devices — we put on our welder's masks, strap ourselves into chairs we've bolted to the floor, take mega-doses of Dramamine, and bring them up on Microsoft's browsers: Internet Explorer (IE) and its new kid brother, Edge.

If the site's fairly simple, the effect is like looking at an eye chart, through a prism, with a really bad hangover. If the site's fairly complex, looking at it in IE/Edge can be like watching film of an explosion at a paint factory in 3D and IMAX while rocketing through the BarfMaster Roller Coaster course at Seven Flags Amusement Park. Either way, it presents challenges.

Have you ever wondered why that is? So have we. This is all we could come up with:

- Microsoft has a morbid fear of web developers becoming complacent. As a result, they pack every new version of IE/Edge with enough quirks and quandaries to keep web developers from ever finishing anything, let alone getting bored.
- Microsoft doesn't see technological progress as being linear. Rather, it sees it as more of a circular firing squad, in which each successive step is killed off, taking coherence, cohesiveness, and continuity with it.
- Microsoft would prefer to be in the Brain Teaser Business, rather than the software business. That's why it forked its own technology (Trident), rather than create something new; rebranded that fork as Edge while keeping the existing IE logo (with minimal modification); continues to chase behind Webkit; and expected anyone to make sense of it, let alone have it render coherently.
- Microsoft believes its users share its apparently huge appetite for risk, which is why it bundles Internet Explorer and Edge with its operating systems. The workforce, after all, can't be bothered to work on systems without any bugs, viruses, malware, spyware, Trojan horses, and myriad malicious mischief.

In any case, if you're a web user — and unless you're a fan of abstract impressionism — you might consider a browser that provides a more visually coherent user experience.

Oh, That's Depressing

It's happened to all of us. We get an email that's so infuriating, or so brutishly stupid, that we respond almost reflexively. We rip off a nasty-gram intended solely for our inner circle, our confidantes, our BFFs, or those poor souls unfortunate enough to be as sarcastic as we are ... only to discover — a nanosecond too late, of course — that we've hit the dreaded Reply All button. Ugh.

That first wave of terror — you know, the one that shoots from your brain to your toes like a bolt of lightning, then roils back up into the pit of your stomach and camps out there — morphs into a morbid, haunting depression. What's worse is you know that depression will never go away until someone invents the Email Eraser and the unintended recipients get amnesia.

Can anything be done? Well, yes. And while it should have been done before you fired off the nasty-gram, it may actually provide some solace post-gaffe.

Fittingly, it comes from a book called, *The Zen Path Through Depression.* Its pertinent advice is this:

> What may be crucial ... is, first, to do nothing. This practice can be difficult because it seems to go against all we believe. Yet to do nothing — to "sit down and shut up" as Katagiri Roshi would say — is the essential practice of Buddhism ... Sometimes, when our back is against the wall, the best thing we can do is to sit down and be quiet.

What we believe, of course, is that we should respond to infuriation and stupidity with a scathing riposte intended to intimidate the offending parties back to the intolerable ignorance whence they came. And we're in no way inclined to say such responses are inappropriate. But since we are, after all, professionals, slightly higher levels of decorum and restraint are typically in fashion.

So, before you let loose the linguistic hellhounds to wreak their savage vengeance on the detestable and the dimwitted — however deserving they may be — take the proverbial deep breath. Step away from the keyboard. Do nothing. Or have a drink. Make it a double, if you will. But give it some time. And if you choose to send the screed anyway, make sure you won't need the bridge you're about to burn to get back across the River Styx.

The depression you save may be your own.

PARDON THE INTERRUPTION

Hi.

We're your programmatic ads.

We show up in everything from websites to apps, from games to online publications, often running on so-called recommendation platforms that monitor your every move on the web and react by trying to sell you stuff the programmatic advertising software thinks you want.

We admit we're stretching the limits of marketing ethics (unless you've already decided that phrase is an oxymoron). But as ads, we're supposed to be opportunistic by nature, aren't we? If you don't want to give us points for that, at least cut us a little slack.

Or how about this? Try looking at us from the standpoint of advertisers or publishers. For them, we're as seductive as Sirens. We create the illusion of having evaluated and reacted to all of their websites' visitors. We make them think they're establishing digital relationships. We let them consider each of these ephemeral relationships a prospect. Then we let them inundate all those anonymous digital connections with ... well ... us.

We know what you're wondering: If the lion's share of those prospects don't buy something — if they never convert into customers — aren't we in hot water? Won't we be accused of falling down on the job? Nope. That's the most amazing thing about being us.

We don't have to actually produce anything, especially results. Why? Because the advertisers and publishers who bet their respective ranches on us aren't counting results. They're counting impressions. Can you believe that? Not conversion rates. Not sales volume. Not incremental revenue. Impressions. If we'd realized it would be this easy, we'd have invented ourselves.

Anyway, now that we have advertisers and publishers buffaloed, our next target is consumers. If we can figure out a way to keep ourselves front and center — to remain on people's screens or apps with no way to get rid of us — we'll take this whole mess to its logical conclusion: Nothing.

That's right. Nothing at all will happen. We'll just sit there. Consumers won't be able to get rid of us or click through. Advertisers and publishers won't even get impressions anymore. And given what they've all fallen for so far, everyone should be happy.

We feel a little selfish saying this. But it's good to be us.

THAT'S BULL

According to *Investopedia*, the terms *bull* and *bear* are used to describe different sets of market conditions. Specifically:

> [Bull] refers to a market that is on the rise. It is typified by a sustained increase in market share prices. In such times, investors have faith that the uptrend will continue in the long term. Typically, the country's economy is strong and employment levels are high … [Bear refers to a market] that is in decline. Share prices are continuously dropping, resulting in a downward trend that investors believe will continue in the long run, which, in turn, perpetuates the spiral. During a bear market, the economy will typically slow down and unemployment will rise as companies begin laying off workers.

Along similar lines, according to BizComics, the term groundhog is used to describe a particular set of business leaders. Specifically:

> [Groundhog] refers to business leaders who engage in the practice of doing the same things over and over again and expecting different results.* Groundhogs are characterized by sustained increases in hope, which they typically mistake for strategy. Groundhogs have faith that whatever success they've achieved will continue in the long term, even if they have no idea how they've achieved it. When the what-me-worry? spending of such faux-successful businesses cause expenses to exceed revenues, the groundhogs who run them will cut marketing, which they consider to be an expense, rather than an investment.

But all of these mammalian metaphors notwithstanding — regardless of whether we're in a bull market or a bear market — the groundhog approach is a recipe for disaster.

If you're committed to doing things the way you've always done them, regardless of how well things seem to be going, you should definitely consider lowering your expectations.* And you might bear a few other things in mind: If you don't market, you can't engage. If you don't engage, you can't sell. If you don't sell, you can't stay in business.

Here's the bottom line: Business is no place for groundhogs. If you think it is, that's bull.

* *Insanity is doing the same thing over and over again and expecting different results.*

GIVE IT UP

Employee benefits sometimes seem like tackling dummies: They get set up, just to get knocked down again and again.

If we consider the history of government-mandated benefits, that may not be so surprising:

> The modern system of getting benefits through a job required another catalyst: World War II ... The government rationed goods even as factories ramped up production and needed to attract workers. Factory owners needed a way to lure employees ... offering more and more generous health plans ... In 1943, the Internal Revenue Service ruled that employer-based health care should be tax

> free. A second law, in 1954, made the tax advantages even more attractive … [starting] from 9 percent of the population in 1940 to 63 percent in 1953.

But in a larger picture, governments are just one particular form of bureaucracy. And bureaucracies are like cats: They're all predictably similar in some aspects and utterly distinct in others. And two of the characteristics shared by all bureaucracies are self-sustenance and the absence of awareness of anything other than sustaining themselves. That's why, in any bureaucracy, the same kind of Q&A is likely to take place:

Q: What do you do?

A: Well, ya see, we process the … uh … hmm … okay … yeah … we're not exactly sure.

Q: Is there a benefit to what you do?

A: We don't know. But it needs to be done.

Q: Why do you do it?

A: Because we've always done it.

Q: Why do you do it the way you do it?

A: Because we've always done it this way.

So, we're left to decide what's worse: the fact that bureaucracies compel us to toil in rote, anonymous invisibility or the fact that effecting change in them is the rough equivalent of turning an aircraft carrier by sticking your hand in the water — you might be able to do it, but it'll take a hell of a long time.

As organisms, it's the nature of bureaucracies to grow and take. Since your benefits may be required to pay the bureaucratic piper, call your tune wisely.

What will you (have to) give up next?

How Do You Spell Spam?

Some people think the Internet is responsible for all the trouble in the world. We're not quite ready to go that far. But it sure has made it easier for people to bother each other.

Case in point: Spam. The term, spam, which refers to unsolicited electronic messages, is reputed to have been adopted from Hormel's canned pig product of the same name. (And why not? The stuff has its own museum, for cryin' out loud.)

Au contraire. The term, SPAM, actually is an acronym, comprising the first letters of this phrase: surveys particularly are malicious. Here's why:

The Internet has spawned a veritable plethora of survey-software sites. Given the ubiquity of the 'Net, you can be sure there's no shortage of users for all of them. And while LinkedIn (the professional/social media platform everyone loves to hate) apparently has opted to eliminate its native surveying capabilities, Facebook does have an app with which you can create custom surveys to annoy your family and friends. One can only imagine:

If I have a particularly heinous gaseous expulsion while driving my car, I should:

A. Call my buddies so we can laugh our asses off.
B. Keep the windows rolled up so I can enjoy it tomorrow.
C. Plug in the cigarette lighter to see if the car explodes.
D. All of the above.
E. None of the above.

If you happen to be one of the odd few who really enjoys SPAM — or even if you're a gastroenterologist — it's not likely you'll find a survey like that particularly constructive or serving some higher purpose. In fact, the Internet Data Investigation Office Testing Service (IDIOTS) recently conducted an independent, constructive, and higher-purpose-serving survey, the results of which indicated most Internet users prefer other activities to receiving SPAM, the top three of which were:

A. Taking a beating
B. Setting themselves on fire
C. Getting in a closed car after a particularly heinous gaseous expulsion.

The IDIOTS survey was conducted on a closed course by professional polltakers. You shouldn't try it at home. And your results may vary. But we strongly suggest you put down the SPAM (and the surveys) and leave your fellow Internet users alone.

SLAPSTICK MEETINGS

We love slapstick comedy as much as anybody. (Maybe more, in fact.) But like everything else, there's a time and a place for it. We love to laugh in meetings, too. But it's better to be laughing with someone than at someone. So, it really makes us wonder why some folks insist on throwing charts in our faces in the hope that said charts will make up for the presenter's disarming lack of substance.

The list is seemingly endless, of course. There are line charts, bar charts, Gantt charts, distribution charts, composition charts, flow charts, process charts, location charts, trend charts, comparison charts, relationship charts, column charts, area charts, scatter charts, bubble charts, surface charts, Cartesian charts, net charts, stock charts, pie charts, donut charts, blueberry popover charts, and our personal favorites — Boston

Cream charts — to say nothing of word clouds and all manner of graphs and diagrams, Venn and otherwise.

But all of that implies a question, which we're irresistibly compelled to ask: Does the fact that you have a pie necessarily mean you have to throw it? If not, and by way of alternatives, here are a few modest suggestions, guaranteed to ensure everyone in attendance at your next meeting is raptly attentive and fully engaged:

- Singing and dancing. Politicians have been using this approach effectively forever.
- Fire walking. As a means of killing time and filling in dead spots in your presentation, this tactic has been used effectively by people as historically and culturally diverse as Brahmin priests, ancient Romans, various and sundry masochists, and Tony Robbins.
- Fill-In-The-Blanks PowerPoint. This interactive exercise is a particular favorite of the collaborative and/or the clueless. If everyone in the meeting is running Windows and using Microsoft Office — and they're all connected via email or an instant messaging app — the participants can contribute charts, graphs, diagrams, and other images using Excel, Visio ... or Draw Free! The presenter, then, can create his slides on the spot, letting the rest of the folks in the room determine the content. It's a real win/win.

As a last resort, if you absolutely have to throw a pie, be it a chart or Vanilla Custard, do it right: Watch the Three Stooges and take notes.

HAVE A HEART

machine (noun)

1. *an apparatus consisting of interrelated parts with separate functions, used in the performance of some kind of work*
2. *a mechanical apparatus or contrivance;* mechanism

"Organization and method mean much, but contagious human characters mean more."
(William James)

Anything that gets big enough becomes self-sustaining: It exists for and unto its own perpetuation. Anything that becomes self-sustaining becomes a machine. Machines are impersonal by definition. They have moving parts. Those parts are interchangeable, replaceable, worthwhile only for their singular functions, vital only to the machine's purpose of self-sustenance. Machines — like monsters and governments — seldom surrender their size, let alone their viability. And they never — ever — look inward ... or back.

That's why, when it comes to our relationships with machines, whether those machines are mechanical or bureaucratic, it always seems like us and them. Does it really have to be like that? No. But the difference comes down to values.

Every organization reflects its leadership (and every monster its creator). If that leadership values the indifferent management of indistinguishable parts, you'll have an organization of crudely equivalent parts, rather than an organization of meaningfully engaged people. If it values mechanical order, you'll have an organization of rote regimentation, rather than an organization of creative adaptation. If it values blind obedience, you'll have an organization of dogmatic, fearful adherence, rather than an organization of mindful allegiance.

On the other hand, if you have a heart — if the leadership of the organization values contribution over conformity, imagination over ingratiation — you just might end up with a passionately committed group of contagious human characters.

Make no mistake: Deliberate, informed sensitivity is more difficult to achieve and sustain than detached, mechanical apathy. Both come with risks.

Before you choose the risk you want, be sure you know the rewards you need.

"But, after all [said the Tin Woodman], brains are not the best things in the world."

"Have you any?" enquired the Scarecrow.

"No, my head is quite empty," answered the Woodman; "but once I had brains, and a heart also; so, having tried them both, I should much rather have a heart."

(L. Frank Baum, *The Wonderful Wizard of Oz*)

BE CAREFUL WHAT YOU ASK FOR

In "How Do You Spell Spam?" we wrote about spam and one of its particular manifestations — surveys. It turns out we may have been a tad shortsighted. That's right. In addition to being annoying for the parties who receive them, particularly if they're unsolicited, surveys also can be troublesome sources of customer dissatisfaction for those who conduct them. Here's why:

Let's say you've invented the proverbial better mousetrap. Let's say it's earned the Good Housekeeping Seal of Approval for its ability to keep your house free from mice, along with their dander, their fleas, their hair, and their droppings. For good measure, let's also say your new mousetrap is approved by PETA because it traps the little varmints without harming or killing them.

Now let's say your contraption sells 20 million units in its first 10 minutes on the market. You're so pumped up from your success that, in an attack of magnanimity, you decide to survey all the people who bought your new trap to find out how they'd want you to improve it.

Finally, let's say the majority of the survey's respondents want you to offer a complementary (and complimentary) service by which you dispatch a vehicle to their homes, pick up the mice they've captured in your traps, transport them to the Humane Society or the local chapter of the ASPCA, and oversee the proper rehabilitation of the little critters now that they've been so mercifully apprehended.

Is this example ludicrous? Of course it is. As a matter of fact, it's deliberately ridiculous. But its point abides: If you ask people to tell you what they want, they will. If you ask people to tell you what they want, they tell you, and you don't give it to them, they'll be royally miffed. At the risk of mixing our mammalian metaphors, if you've already achieved success, your best met may be to let sleeping dogs lie. At the very least, be careful what you ask for.

If you opt not to be careful, be prepared to staff up your complaint center.

Don't Be So Literal

As creators of messages, we know our communications have to be clear, precise, and (as much as practicable) free from ambiguity, equivocation, and obfuscation. But reason (and sanity) suggests there should be limits. (Please!)

Here are a few examples of instances in which the speaker (or writer) might be cut some degree of slack:

- "I'll have that done in two seconds." Unless the person from whom this comment came was referring to blinking, snapping his fingers, or throwing back a shot of Bushmills on St. Patrick's Day, we can all agree to take this one with a grain of salt.

- "Take this with a grain of salt." Chances are that even habitual users of this expression don't walk around with packets of Morton in their pockets — unless they're trying to keep themselves from being poisoned or trying to stave off a hangover from too many shots of Bushmills.
- "Man, when I lifted that thing, it weighed a ton!" If this expression is used by The Incredible Hulk, it's probably okay to take it literally. If not, most of us would be fairly safe taking it with a grain of salt. (A shot of Bushmills wouldn't hurt, either.)
- "That guy's dumb as a rock." For its ostensible sarcasm, its overt absurdity, and its seeming impossibility, this expression could almost be eliminated or ignored entirely — with one exception. And when it comes to that guy, there isn't enough salt or Bushmills on the planet.
- "He's as strong as an ox." Since the only ox whose feats of physical power have been meaningfully documented is Babe, it takes a little imagination to even formulate a rudimentary conception of the meaning of this saying. In our experience, we've always found such imaginings to be enhanced by copious amounts of Bushmills (with or without the salt), especially if we're accompanied by an imbiber with the prodigious capacity of Paul Bunyan.
- "He drinks like a fish." This one's immediately dismissible since, unless he's as large as Paul Bunyan, no one could drink that much — whether he's drinking Bushmills or anything else.

We don't care if you hang on our every word. Just don't be so literal.

JUMP!

We can't help but notice more and more people lining up to tell more and more people how to do more and more things. It seems as if every public nuisance with a keyboard or a microphone is out to tell someone what to do or how to do it. And the really obnoxious ones make lists.

That's why we're constantly seeing things like these:

- The Top Ten Reasons Why You Should Take That Job
- The Top Ten Reasons Why You Shouldn't Take That Job
- The Top Ten Reasons Why You Should Have a Job
- The Top Ten Reasons Why You Don't Need a Job

- The Top Ten Things You Should Do If You Don't Have a Job
- The Top Ten Things You Should Never Do If You Don't Have a Job
- The Top Ten Reasons Why You Should Have a Job If You're Going to Look For a Job
- The Top Ten Reasons Why You Shouldn't Have a Job If You're Going to Look For a Job
- The Top Ten Reasons Finding a Job Should Be Your Job If You Don't Have a Job
- The Top Ten Reasons Why You Shouldn't Have a Job If You Intend to Make Looking for a Job Your Job If You Don't Have a Job.

We think this kind of vapid nonsense is the single biggest argument in favor of entrepreneurialism. Here's why:

If you're Party C, we can't understand the logic by which Party A would employ Party B to tell you what to do. By the same token, we can't understand why so many public nuisances could presume to know you well enough to tell you what to do.

Are they smarter than you are? Not likely. Are they more capable than you are? Probably not. Will Party B commit his political allegiance to you or to Party A? See *Hierarchy, Corporate.* If Parties A and B or the public nuisances weren't around, would you be incapable of functioning? We doubt it. And in the bigger picture, does the notion of job security even exist anymore? Not as far as we can see.

Bottom line? Trust yourself.

You may have to jump off the ledge. But it doesn't mean you won't land on your feet.

About the Authors

After failing to distinguish himself in any way at all during his K-12 years, Mark O'Brien took 10 years off to pursue his dream of becoming a rock star. (It didn't go well.) During that time, he supported himself with prestigious positions such as hospital orderly, truck driver for a construction company, clothing salesman, and warehouseman for an appliance distributor. Waking one morning to realize he was getting neither younger nor smarter, he got his sorry keister to school, earning a B.A. in English Literature from Trinity College in Hartford, CT. Since writing was the only thing he was sure he could do since discovering Stan Lee's Marvel Comics at age 10, Mark plied his trade at insurance companies, a public relations agency, and an advertising agency before deciding to be his own boss. You can learn more about Mark and what he does on his website — obriencg.com. And you can find his other writing on Amazon by entering Mark Nelson O'Brien in the search field.

After selling his first cartoon in 5th grade (for five bucks), Nate Fakes used it to try to impress a 6th-grade girl. It didn't work. Giving up on 6th-grade girls but not cartooning, Nate spent his middle- and high-school years drawing all day (instead of paying attention in class). He made such a name for himself with his edgy humor, his high-school principal invited him to stop drawing cartoons that poked fun at people, or he wouldn't be invited to graduate. Nate accepted. At Wright State University in Dayton, OH, he was the graphic artist and cartoonist for the school newspaper, *The Guardian.* That gig landed him an internship at *MAD* in New York City, writing for the magazine and cleaning the storage room. At the end of the internship, with the storage room all spiffy, Nate returned to Ohio, worked with *MAD* on three different series, and started selling and syndicating his own work. You can learn more about Nate and see more of his work on his website — natefakescartoons.com.

77112914R00042

Made in the USA
San Bernardino, CA
19 May 2018